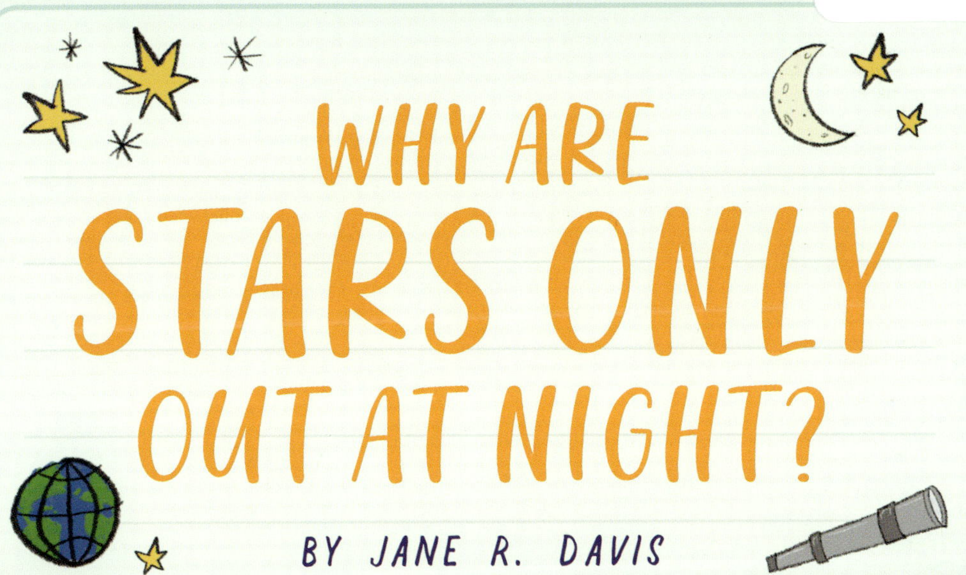

WHY ARE STARS ONLY OUT AT NIGHT?

BY JANE R. DAVIS

Please visit our website, www.enslow.com. For a free color catalog of all our high-quality books, call toll free 1-800-398-2504 or fax 1-877-980-4454.

Library of Congress Cataloging-in-Publication Data
Names: Davis, Jane R., author.
Title: Why are stars only out at night? / Jane R. Davis.
Description: Buffalo, New York : Enslow Publishing, [2026] | Series: Earth science explorers | Includes bibliographical references and index. | Audience: Grades K-1
Identifiers: LCCN 2024058624 (print) | LCCN 2024058625 (ebook) | ISBN 9781978543652 (library binding) | ISBN 9781978543645 (paperback) | ISBN 9781978543669 (ebook)
Subjects: LCSH: Stars–Juvenile literature.
Classification: LCC QB801.7 .D38 2026 (print) | LCC QB801.7 (ebook) | DDC 523.8–dc23/eng/20250101
LC record available at https://lccn.loc.gov/2024058624
LC ebook record available at https://lccn.loc.gov/2024058625

Published in 2026 by
Enslow Publishing
2544 Clinton Street
Buffalo, NY 14224

Designer: Claire Zimmermann
Editor: Kristen Nelson

Photo credits: Cover (girl) Krakenimages.com/Shutterstock.com, (night sky photo) Dudarev Mikhail/ Shutterstock.com; series art (composition book texture) notebook-texture/Shutterstock.com, (tape) pics five/Shutterstock.com, (doodles and illustrations used throughout) Claire Zimmermann; p. 5 Bilanol/Shutterstock.com; p. 7 yusufdemirci/Shutterstock.com; p. 9 Utthapon wiratepsupon/ Shutterstock.com; p. 11 Yurii_Yarema/Shutterstock.com; p. 13 yamasan0708/Shutterstock.com; p. 15 Terrance Emerson/Shutterstock.com; p. 17 marcin jucha/Shutterstock.com; p. 19 AstroStar/ Shutterstock.com; p. 21 Vasilyev Alexandr/Shutterstock.com.

Printed in the United States of America

Some of the images in this book illustrate individuals who are models. The depictions do not imply actual situations or events.

CPSIA compliance information: Batch #CSENS26: For further information contact Enslow Publishing, at 1-800-398-2504.

CONTENTS

BOLDFACE WORDS APPEAR IN THE GLOSSARY

SKY AT NIGHT

Have you ever looked up at the sky and seen stars? It was likely nighttime when you did this! If you look into the sky around noon, you wouldn't be able to see stars. Let's find out why this is!

YOU DON'T NEED ANY SPECIAL TOOLS TO SEE THE STARS IN THE NIGHT SKY.

THE SUN

The sun is the source of light and heat on Earth. It is the closest star to Earth. It's a star we can see during the day! When it is night somewhere on Earth, that part of the planet is facing away from the sun.

NIGHT

DAY

EARTH ROTATES, OR SPINS. ONE FULL SPIN IS EQUAL TO ABOUT 24 HOURS, OR ONE DAY.

STAR FACTS

The stars we see only at night are much farther away from Earth than the sun. Their light is not as bright or strong. The closer a star is, the brighter it will look to us.

STARS ARE DIFFERENT SIZES. VERY OFTEN, THE BIGGER THE STAR, THE BRIGHTER IT LOOKS TO US.

9

THE BRIGHTEST!

Our sun shines brightly during the day. It shines so brightly that it blocks the light of all the other stars! That means that even during the day, the stars are there. We just can't see them!

OUR SUN ISN'T THE BIGGEST STAR IN OUR **GALAXY**. IT LOOKS LARGE TO US BECAUSE IT'S SO CLOSE!

WHAT'S THAT TWINKLE?

There are **billions** of stars. You only see about 2,000 when looking at the night sky. Stars look like they twinkle, or change brightness a little, at times. The wind and **temperature** differences in Earth's **atmosphere** cause this, not the stars themselves.

HAVE YOU EVER HEARD OF A SHOOTING STAR? IT'S NOT A STAR! IT'S A METEOR, OR SPACE ROCK BURNING UP IN EARTH'S ATMOSPHERE.

VENUS RISING

You may see a light in the sky just before the sun rises or just after it sets. This isn't a star! It's the planet Venus. Because of when it appears in the sky, it may be called the morning star or the evening star.

VENUS

LONG AGO, PEOPLE THOUGHT THE MORNING STAR AND EVENING STAR WERE TWO DIFFERENT **CELESTIAL** BODIES.

OTHER PLANETS

Other planets in our solar system can be seen in the night sky among the stars. Mercury, Mars, Jupiter, and Saturn are possible to spot. You can tell the light is a planet, not a star, because it won't twinkle like a star does.

THIS PICTURE SHOWS VENUS, JUPITER, AND MERCURY IN THE NIGHT SKY.

TIME TO STARGAZE!

Now that you know why stars are only out at night, it's time to go see them! The best nights to stargaze, or look at stars, are those without clouds. Aim for a night with little moonlight too. Go to a place away from streetlights, cars, and houses if you can.

ALWAYS HAVE A GROWN-UP WITH YOU WHEN YOU STARGAZE AT NIGHT.

It takes about a half an hour for your eyes to get used to the darkness. Then, look up! You should see the beauty of many stars in the sky. You can use a telescope to help you see them even better.

A TELESCOPE IS A TOOL THAT MAKES FARAWAY OBJECTS LOOK BIGGER AND CLOSER.

GLOSSARY

atmosphere: The mixture of gases that surround a planet.

billion: 1,000 million, or 1,000,000,000.

celestial: Having to do with the sky.

galaxy: A large group of stars, planets, gas, and dust that form a unit within the universe.

temperature: How hot or cold something is.

FOR MORE INFORMATION

BOOKS

Walpole, Brenda. *I Wonder Why the Sun Rises: and Other Questions About Time and Seasons.* London, UK: Kingfisher, 2023.

Wilsher, Jane. *My First Space Atlas.* San Rafeal, CA: EarthAware Kids, 2023.

WEBSITES

Astronomy for Kids

https://www.amnh.org/explore/ology/astronomy

Do you want to know more about the science of stars? Check out this website for kids.

Stars

https://science.nasa.gov/universe/stars/

Check out more about what stars are made up of here.

INDEX

TITLES IN THIS SERIES

WHAT MAKES RAINBOWS APPEAR?	WHY ARE DAYS LONGER IN SUMMER?	WHY ARE STARS ONLY OUT AT NIGHT?
WHY DOES IT RAIN AND SNOW?	WHY DOES THE SUN RISE AND SET?	WHY IS EARTH ROUND?

ISBN: 9781978543645